moms in prayer
INTERNATIONAL™
Praying for Children and Schools

The Moms in Prayer
Booklet

by Fern Nichols
President/Founder
Moms in Prayer International

All you need to know to start or join a group!

Notice

No portion of this publication may be translated into any language
or reproduced in any form, except for brief quotations, without prior
written permission of the author.

Copyright © 1987 Fern Nichols. All rights reserved.
First to sixteenth printings, 1987-2009.
Seventeenth printing, September 2012 revised from
Moms In Touch International to Moms in Prayer International.
Printed in the United States of America.
ISBN 978-1-929477-17-3

Moms in Prayer International
P.O. Box 1120, Poway, California 92074-1120, USA

Phone: 858.486.4065
e-mail: info@MomsInPrayer.org
www.MomsInPrayer.org

Table of Contents

Introduction

*M*y heart was heavy as I sent my two eldest children to their first day of public junior high school. That fall day in 1984, I was burdened with concern for the new world they were entering. I knew they would face their greatest test in resisting immoral values, vulgar language and peer pressure. My heart cried out to the Lord asking Him to protect them, to enable them to see clearly the difference between right and wrong, and to guide them in making good decisions.

The burden to intercede for my boys was so overwhelming that I knew I could not bear it alone. I asked God to give me another mom who felt the same burden and who would be willing to pray with me concerning our children and their school. God heard the cry of my heart and led me to phone another mom who voiced her agreement as I shared my burden. We also thought of a few other moms who might want to pray with us. We called them and began meeting for prayer the following week.

This was the beginning of the interdenominational, Christian prayer movement Moms in Prayer International (formerly known as Moms In Touch). As moms began sharing what God had been doing in their lives, and in the lives of their children because of prayer, other groups began to spring up all over British Columbia where we were living at the time. Groups formed for elementary through high school levels. The initial material in this *Booklet* was formulated during that year. What a thrill to see God's plan unfold!

The summer of 1985 brought a change to our family as we moved from Abbotsford, British Columbia, to Poway, California. I soon discovered that God was giving me still greater opportunities for carrying on the work that began in Canada. I prayed God would raise up moms who were willing to intercede for their children.

God has been faithful to send us women who will pray. Moms in Prayer groups now meet in every state in the USA and in more than 140 other countries. Because moms were asking how to pray and how to begin a Moms in Prayer group, we created this *Booklet*.

I would like to acknowledge Sondra Ball, who helped me compile this material. Her encouragement, suggestions, time, friendship and loving support have been specific answers to my prayers.

I pray that God will raise up moms to intercede for every school in our nation and around the world. What a thrilling thought to consider two or more moms gathered together every week in prayer for their children and their schools.

Let me challenge you to be involved in your child's life through prayer. See what God can do for your children and their schools when you are faithful to pray with at least one other mom on a regular basis.

Believing in the power of God through prayer,

Fern Nichols

Fern Nichols

Arise, cry out in the night,
at the beginning of the night watches!
Pour out your heart like water
before the presence of the Lord!
Lift your hands to him
for the lives of your children,
who faint for hunger
at the head of every street.

Lamentations 2:19 (ESV)

Fern's Testimony

J would like to share how God has worked in my personal life regarding prayer. Many years ago, I was asked to speak at a prayer retreat which resulted in a serious evaluation of my prayer life. Listening to several tapes on prayer by Ron Dunn helped me greatly. I also read wonderful books on prayer, but I knew within my heart that listening to discussions about prayer, talking about prayer, or reading about prayer didn't make up for my lack of actually praying.

I seemed to always be praying "on the run." My prayer time was hit and miss. God, in His grace, allowed me to see that my priorities were not right. I was busy being productive in many wonderful things, but I wasn't doing the best thing—spending consistent prayer time with my Heavenly Father.

I believe Satan has us thinking that being spiritual means being productive. He doesn't want us to cross over the invisible line into powerful, intercessory prayer. If he can keep us thinking that being on the productive side of the line is doing great things for God, then we will secure few blessings for our family, schools, community and nation. But if we recognize the line and cross over it to be intercessors, God will move heaven and earth to answer our prayers, and we will begin to see great victories and Satan's defeat. Satan trembles when he sees the weakest saint on her knees, for he knows he has no power against our prayers that are prayed according to God's will.

Here is a list of what I asked God to do in my life in this matter of prayer.

- ✌ That I would be a woman of prayer
- ✌ That I would gain a vision for the power of God through prayer
- ✌ That I would seek to become an intercessor
- ✌ That I would begin to practice proactive praying, taking the initiative to pray with others as a way of life
- ✌ That I would learn to pray using the Scriptures
- ✌ That I would pray without ceasing
- ✌ That I would be able to communicate to others what God is teaching me in prayer

If the Holy Spirit is speaking to your heart as you read this list, stop right now, heed His voice and pray.

I believe the ministry of prayer is the highest calling a Christian can have. Right now, Jesus is seated at the right hand of God interceding for you (Romans 8:34).

I believe the ministry of prayer is the highest calling a Christian can have.

—Fern Nichols

Mission Statement

Moms in Prayer International impacts children and schools worldwide for Christ by gathering mothers to pray.

Vision Statement

Our vision is that every school in the world would be covered with prayer.

Moms In Touch International changed its name to
Moms in Prayer International in January 2012.
The mission and vision of the ministry remain the same.
Only the name has changed.

Purpose

- To stand in the gap for our children through prayer

- To pray that our children will receive Jesus as Lord and Savior, then stand boldly in their faith

- To pray for teachers and staff

- To pray that teachers, administrators, staff and students will come to faith in Jesus Christ

- To pray that our schools will be directed by biblical values and high moral standards

- To be an encouragement and a positive support to our schools

- To provide hope and strength to moms who carry heavy burdens for their children

What is Moms in Prayer?

Two or more women who meet regularly
(one hour a week is optimal) to intercede on behalf
of children and schools through prayer

Christian mothers, grandmothers or any woman
who is willing to pray for a specific child and school

Women who believe that God answers prayer!

Starting a Group

ࢶ Pray that God brings you another mom willing to meet with
you each week for prayer.

ࢶ Read and agree with the Moms in Prayer Statement of Faith.

ࢶ Use the Moms in Prayer Four Steps of Prayer format.

ࢶ Abide by the Policies of the ministry.

ࢶ Make a list of prospective moms from your school and ask them
to join your prayer time.

ࢶ Visit www.MomsInPrayer.org/Leaders Corner to register your
group or fill out and return the Registration Form at the back of
this *Booklet*. This will enable us to refer interested moms to your
group, as well as send news and updates from the ministry.

ࢶ Encourage each group member to register online or mail in the
Registration Form at the back of the *Moms in Prayer Booklet*.

ࢶ Visit www.MomsInPrayer.org/Leaders Corner for Prayer Sheets
and other helpful tools to enhance your prayer hour.

ࢶ Trust God for answers to prayer, focus on Him and expect great
things to happen.

Helpful Suggestions for Your Group

As you begin:

- ॐ Come as you are.

- ॐ Be faithful in meeting for one hour on a regular basis (weekly is optimal). Stress the importance of faithful commitment to the group. Regular attendance develops consistent prayer coverage, builds trust, instills unity and strengthens the group.

- ॐ Start and finish on time.

- ॐ Read the *Moms in Prayer Booklet* periodically.

- ॐ Avoid distractions by not serving refreshments.

- ॐ Place a "Please Do Not Disturb" note on the door and silence all phones.

Each mom needs:

- ॐ A Bible

- ॐ Her own *Moms in Prayer Booklet*

- ॐ Someone to care for her children if they are not in school during this hour

In matters of prayer:

- ॐ Pray conversationally in One Accord using the Four Steps of Prayer format.

- ॐ Do not get sidetracked in talking about your requests: Pray about them. Share your thanksgivings and requests in prayer rather than discussing them first.

- ॐ **Keep everything that is said or prayed in a Moms in Prayer meeting confidential.** Nothing said should ever be shared with anyone outside of that group. Confidentiality cannot be overemphasized.

Praying in One Accord
Method of Prayer

*C*onversationally praying in one accord is the method of prayer that is used in our Moms in Prayer groups. One accord prayer is agreeing together as directed and energized by the Holy Spirit. When a group prays in one accord, they concentrate on **one subject at a time.** More than one mom can pray on each subject until that subject is covered.

Do not be concerned about silence; God also speaks during these times. Try to keep prayers **short** and **simple.** This will encourage everyone to participate.

In her book *What Happens When Women Pray*, Evelyn Christenson says, "When people start praying together in one accord, to our Father in heaven, in the name of Jesus, and practice praying together, things begin to change. Our lives change, our families change, our school, church and communities change. Changes take place not when we study about prayer, not when we talk about it, not even when we memorize beautiful Scripture verses on prayer. It is when we actually pray that things begin to happen."

If you have never prayed conversationally before, please do not feel you must pray aloud. You may pray silently. The more you experience conversational prayer, the easier it will be for you to eventually join in.

By praying in one accord, we hear the heartfelt thoughts of others, and echo those words in our hearts as well. This will cause us to focus on Almighty God and not on ourselves. He will give you the words to say. The eloquence of your prayer is not what is important. **The sincerity of your heart is what God hears.**

Prayer Time
Format: Four Steps of Prayer
The Moms in Prayer hour is divided into Four Steps of Prayer:
Praise, Confession, Thanksgiving and Intercession.

To ensure plenty of time to thoroughly pray for your children, school and staff, we estimate about 25 minutes for Praise, Confession and Thanksgiving, and about 35 minutes devoted to Intercession.

*P*raise. Every prayer time begins with praising God for His characteristics using His Word. Our faith becomes strong as we pray back to God what He says about Himself, praising Him for who He is and not for what He has done—no answers to prayer or requests during this time. This is God's time.

The following illustrates the method of praising God in one accord. A leader chooses an attribute (a characteristic) of God, for example, Shepherd. Select verses that reflect the attribute, such as Psalm 23:1 and Isaiah 40:11. Read them aloud. Psalm 23:1 (NASB), *The Lord is my shepherd, I shall not want.* Then read Isaiah 40:11 (NLT), *He will feed his flock like a shepherd. He will carry the lambs in his arms, holding them close to his heart. He will gently lead the mother sheep with their young.*

After reading the verses aloud, the group leader begins by praying, "Father, I praise You that You are a God who meets every need of your children, like a shepherd providing for his sheep."

Another mom might continue by praying, "I agree, Lord. I rejoice that You care for us so deeply. Just as a shepherd knows his sheep, You know our needs."

A third mom might pray, "We praise You for giving us this beautiful picture of Yourself as our Shepherd, One who understands us and carries us in Your arms, holding us close to Your heart."

Praising God as the Shepherd continues until the subject is completely covered.

Additional Attributes of God

Faithful—Deuteronomy 7:9; Psalm 145:13; II Timothy 2:13

Wise—Isaiah 55:8-9; Daniel 2:20-22; Romans 11:33-34

Eternal—Psalm 90:2; Daniel 7:14; Revelation 1:8, 18

Compassionate—Psalm 103:13-14; Isaiah 30:18-19; Matthew 9:36

Holy—Exodus 15:11; Isaiah 57:15; Revelation 15:4

Creator—Jeremiah 10:12; Psalm 95:3-6; Colossians 1:16

More Attributes of God can be found in the *Leader's Guide & Personal Prayer Time*

As we praise God:

- ☙ It exalts God and gives Him glory.
- ☙ It is declaring, proclaiming, confessing who God is.
- ☙ It is for our good. It brings freedom and encouragement to our lives because we focus on God and not our situation.
- ☙ It brings about an awareness of His Presence (Psalm 22:3).
- ☙ It dispels the enemy's power, and he is defeated. From II Chronicles 20:22 (NKJV), *Now when they began to sing and to praise ... [the enemy was] defeated.*

Confession. Following your time of praise, God may reveal some areas of your life that are not pleasing to Him. The group leader invites each member to take a few moments to silently confess those sins to God. Isaiah 59:2 (AMP) tells us, *But your iniquities have made a separation between you and your God, and your sins have hidden His face from you, so that He will not hear.* God says that He will not answer our prayer if there is unconfessed sin. Our relationship must not only be right with Him, but also with others, if we desire God to hear and answer our prayers.

How do we confess our sin when convicted by the Holy Spirit?

1. Name the sin specifically, agreeing with God that it is sin.
2. Repent concerning the sin. This will result in changed attitudes and actions.

3. Thank God that He has forgiven your sin because of what Christ did on the cross. I John 1:9 (KJV), *If we confess our sins, he is faithful and just to forgive us our sins, and to cleanse us from all unrighteousness.*

4. Ask to be filled and controlled by the Holy Spirit. Surrender your will and make a total commitment of yourself to God.

   ~ Command—Ephesians 5:18b (NASB), *Be filled with the Spirit.*

   ~ Promise—I John 5:14-15 (NASB), *This is the confidence which we have before Him, that, if we ask anything according to His will, He hears us. And if we know that He hears us in whatever we ask, we know that we have the requests which we have asked from Him.*

5. By faith, thank Him that He has filled you on the basis of His promise. Do not depend on your feelings. The promise of God's Word, not our feelings, is our authority.

*T*hanksgiving. During this time, we offer prayers of thanksgiving, expressing appreciation and gratefulness for God's answers to our prayers. In I Thessalonians 5:18 (KJV), the Apostle Paul exhorts, *In everything give thanks: for this is the will of God in Christ Jesus concerning you.* In Psalm 50:23a (NASB), God's Word tells us that when we give thanks we honor Him: *He who offers a sacrifice of thanksgiving honors Me.*

Instead of spending time telling the answer to your prayer, pray the answer. The other moms will join in one accord, agreement prayer, thanking God with you. Here is an example.

First mom: "Dear Father, thank You that my son has found a Christian friend at school."

Second mom: "Thank You for Your perfect timing. You knew how lonely he was, that he needed a Christian friend to help him be strong in You."

Third mom: "We thank You, Father, for Your goodness and that You truly care about every detail of his life."

When one subject is finished, another mom can introduce the next answer to prayer and so on.

Be sure to dedicate this time to thanksgiving only. It will be tempting to mention requests, but remember to focus on giving thanks.

*I*ntercession. This is a powerful prayer time as we come to God interceding on behalf of children, teachers and staff, school concerns and Moms in Prayer. If your group is large, we suggest you divide into smaller groups of two or three, allowing more time to pray for each child.

Children. The leader shares a Scripture verse to pray for the children. As we pray, placing our child's name in the verse, the power of God's Word drives out anxiety and fear, and produces faith in us. Remember that faith is taking God at His word and acting accordingly. It is accepting God's words no matter what the circumstances or how we feel.

Here is an example of praying in one accord for our children using Colossians 1:10 (NASB), *May _____ (add child's name) walk in a manner worthy of the Lord, pleasing Him in all respects, bearing fruit in every good work and increasing in the knowledge of God.*

First mom: "Dear Father, I ask that David will live a life worthy of the Lord and please You in every way, bearing fruit in every good work, growing in the knowledge of God."

Second mom: "Yes, Father, I ask that David will conduct himself the way a Christian should, no matter how difficult the circumstances."

Third mom: "Dear Lord, I agree with these prayers and ask that David will not live one way at home and church, and another way at school. I ask that his Christian walk would be a part of every aspect of his life."

Second mom: "And Father, that You will open his eyes to what really pleases You, that he will know that obedience brings blessings."

Cover all prayer thoughts from this verse for David before going on to the next child. Pray for each child using this Scripture verse before praying a specific request.

After you have prayed scripturally for each child, pray for a specific need of each child, such as salvation, a concern with a teacher, grades, the salvation of friends, choice of friends or communication at home, etc. You may record these requests on the Prayer Sheet. (A blank Prayer Sheet is in the center of the *Moms in Prayer Booklet* for you to copy and use.)

Prayer Suggestions for Our Children

Pray for their relationship with God.

- ھ That they may know the unconditional love of God (Ephesians 3:18-19)
- ھ That at an early age they may accept Jesus Christ as their Savior (II Timothy 3:15)
- ھ That they will allow God to work in their lives to accomplish His purposes for them (Philippians 2:13)
- ھ That they will earnestly seek God and love to go to church (Psalm 63:1; Psalm 122:1)
- ھ That they will be caught when guilty (Numbers 32:23)

Pray for godly attributes.

- ھ That they will be protected from attitudes of inferiority or superiority (Genesis 1:27; Philippians 2:3)
- ھ That they will respect authority (I Peter 2:13-14)
- ھ That they will be the best students they can be (Colosians 3:23)
- ھ That they will hate sin (Psalm 97:10)
- ھ That they will control their tempers (Ephesians 4:26)
- ھ That they will exhibit the fruit of the Spirit in their lives (Galatians 5:22-23)

Pray for relationships with family.

- ھ That they will obey their parents in the Lord (Proverbs 1:8; Colossians 3:20)
- ھ That they will accept discipline and profit from it (Proverbs 3:11-12)
- ھ That they will love their siblings and not allow rivalry to hinder lifelong, positive relationships (Ephesians 4:32)

Pray for relationships with friends.

- ھ That unsaved friends will come to know Jesus (II Peter 3:9)
- ھ That they will choose godly friends, who will build them up in the Lord, and be kept from harmful friendships that will lead them astray (Ecclesiastes 4:10; Proverbs 1:10)

- That they will be firm in their convictions and withstand peer pressure (Ephesians 4:14; I Corinthians 15:33)
- That they will be friends to the lonely, the discouraged, the lost (Matthew 25:40; Philippians 2:4)

Pray for protection.

- From the evil one (John 17:15)
- From drugs, alcohol and tobacco (Proverbs 20:1; 23:31-32)
- From victimization and molestation (Luke 17:1-2)
- From premarital sex (I Corinthians 6:18-20)
- From physical danger, accidents and illnesses (Philippians 4:6)

Pray for their future.

- That they will seek God when choosing a spouse (II Corinthians 6:14)
- That they will be wise in the choice of a career (Proverbs 3:6)
- That they will use their God-given gifts, talents and abilities for His glory (Matthew 25:21; Ephesians 2:10)

More Scriptures to pray for your children:

Deuteronomy 10:12-13	Ephesians 1:18-19	Philippians 3:10	II Timothy 2:15-16
I Chronicles 28:9	Ephesians 4:1-2	Colossians 1:9-11	James 4:8
Matthew 6:33	Ephesians 4:23-25a	Colossians 2:6-8	I John 1:8-9
John 17:26	Ephesians 4:29	Colossians 3:1-2	I John 2:15-16
Romans 12:2	Ephesians 5:1-3	I Thessalonians 4:3-4,7	I John 3:7

Prayer Suggestions for Teachers & Staff

As we pray for teachers and staff, we can be confident that God is hearing and answering our prayers, even though we might not see the results.

Many teachers have shared how much they have appreciated and counted on our prayers. One teacher, with tears in her eyes, expressed that she couldn't believe we would actually take the time and have the concern to pray for her. She thought the only other person who ever prayed for her was her mom.

Begin by praying a Scripture for the teachers/staff:

II Chronicles 19:7	II Corinthians 9:8	Philippians 1:9-11	I Timothy 6:20
Psalm 43:3	Ephesians 1:17	Colossians 3:12-15	II Timothy 2:24-25
Proverbs 2:10-11	Ephesians 3:18-19	Colossians 3:17	Titus 2:7
I Corinthians 4:2	Ephesians 6:19-20	Colossians 4:3-6	I Peter 5:2

Specific prayer suggestions for teachers:

> ☞ Pray they will accept God's gift of salvation.

> ☞ Pray they will teach with excellence and creativity.

> ☞ Pray they will use speech that is gracious and pleasant.

> ☞ Pray they will consider each child as a special individual, not just as "their class" or "their job."

> ☞ Pray they will have the zeal to make a difference for good in each student's life.

> ☞ Pray they will not grow weary in doing good (Galatians 6:9), that their commitment to excellence and discipline will not wane.

> ☞ Pray substitute teachers will be able to control classrooms and be a welcome and positive influence.

> ☞ Pray those teachers going through difficult personal problems will seek God.

> ☞ Pray Christian teachers will recognize secular philosophies within the curriculum and openly stand firm in their values.

Prayer Suggestions for Schools

As we pray for school concerns, we intercede for God's power to impact our child's school environment.

> ☞ Pray that positions at the national, state and local level will be filled by men and women with godly principles and values.

> ☞ Pray that new curriculum will be chosen wisely and that it will include biblical standards and high moral values.

> ☞ Pray that each student will learn of God's great love and provision for salvation, and accept God's forgiving grace.

> ☞ Pray that children from difficult family situations will receive godly counsel and compassion from their teachers.

Prayer Sheet

- Copy the Prayer Sheet for each member of your group
- Start on time
- Materials needed: Bible, *Moms in Prayer Booklet*, pen

moms in prayer
INTERNATIONAL
Praying for Children and Schools

Date _____

Praise—Praising God for **who He is,** His attributes, His name or His character.
Please no answers to prayer or prayer requests during this time.

Attribute: _____

Definition: _____

Scripture(s): _____

_____

Thoughts: _____

Confession—Silently confessing sins to the God who forgives.
I John 1:9, *If we confess our sins, he is faithful and just and will forgive us our sins and purify us from all unrighteousness.*

Thanksgiving—Thanking God for **what He has done.** *Please no prayer requests during this time.*
I Thessalonians 5:18, *In everything give thanks; for this is God's will for you in Christ Jesus.*

Intercession—Coming to God in prayer on behalf of others. *Form groups of two or three.*

Child #1 _____

Child #2 _____

Child #3 _____

Specific Request

Child #1 _____

Child #2 _____

Child #3 _____

Teachers/Staff

Scripture Open _____ 's eyes so he/she may turn from darkness to light and from the dominion of Satan to God, that he/she may receive forgiveness of sins and an inheritance among those who have been sanctified by faith in Jesus Christ. (From Acts 26:18 NASB)

Specific Request: _____

School Concerns: _____

Moms in Prayer Concerns: _____

Remember, what is prayed in the group, stays in the group!

- Pray that your school will be drug-free and alcohol-free and no addictions will have hold on the youth.
- Pray that God will protect students against unwise choices in extracurricular activities.
- Pray that there will be respect for one another, regardless of race or religion.
- Pray for every child in the school by name, if possible. (Yearbooks are helpful for this.)
- Pray protection for the school campus.

Prayer Suggestions for Moms in Prayer International

As you close your prayer time, take a few minutes to pray for the ministry of Moms in Prayer International. For specific requests for the ministry visit www.MomsInPrayer.org/LeadersCorner/MinistryRequests.

- Pray for other moms to join your group.
- Pray for each school (by name) in your district to have a Moms in Prayer group.
- Pray for a group for every school in your city or immediate area.
- Pray that every school in your state will have a Moms in Prayer group.
- Pray that every nation around the world will have moms praying for their children and schools.
- Pray that the Lord will give the Moms in Prayer staff and board of directors wisdom and discernment in all decisions they must make on behalf of this ministry.
- Pray that God will keep the ministry pure and untarnished.

To facilitate following the Four Step of Prayer, you may use the Prayer Sheet that has been inserted into the center of the *Moms in Prayer Booklet*. This can be reproduced and used as your master copy. Prayer Sheet forms are also available at www.MomsInPrayer.org/LeadersCorner/PrayerSheets. You can download a Prayer Sheet document and fill in an attribute and verses of your choosing, or you can download one of our 52 partially filled-in Prayer Sheets featuring an attribute of God and corresponding verses.

Praying for the Nonbeliever

*W*hen someone's salvation seems impossible, we need to believe by faith the verse Mark 10:27b (KJV), *With God all things are possible.* We are in a spiritual battle. Thank God that our spiritual weapons are mighty and our authority in Christ is far above the rulers, powers and forces of darkness. The enemy must yield (II Corinthians 10:3-5). We pray in the name of Jesus, asking for the salvation of students, teachers and staff members. This takes faith, patience and persistence. Remember II Corinthians 5:7 (NASB), *For we walk by faith, not by sight.*

Here is an example of one accord prayer for the nonbeliever using II Corinthians 10:3-5:

First mom: "Dear Father, in the name of the Lord Jesus, we pray for the tearing down of all the works of Satan in the life of Sarah."

Second mom: "We pray that her very thoughts will be brought into captivity to the obedience of Christ."

Third mom: "With the authority of the name of the Lord Jesus Christ, we ask for Sarah's deliverance from the power and persuasions of the evil one."

First mom: "We pray that her conscience will be convicted, and that You, God, will bring her to the point of repentance, and that Sarah will listen and believe as she hears or reads the Word of God."

Third mom: "May Your perfect will and purpose be accomplished in and through Sarah."

With God all things are possible.
Mark 10:27b (KJV)

20

Promises to Claim

*S*uggested Scriptures to study and incorporate in your prayer time for nonbelievers:

Ezekiel 11:19	I Corinthians 4:3-4	Mark 1:5
I Timothy 2:4-6	John 14:6	II Timothy 2:25-26
Romans 10:13-15	II Peter 3:9	

II Chronicles 7:14 (NKJV), *If My people who are called by My name will humble themselves, and pray and seek My face, and turn from their wicked ways, then I will hear from heaven, and will forgive their sin and heal their land.*

Psalm 44:5 (NKJV), *Through You we will push down our enemies; Through Your name we will trample those who rise up against us.*

Psalm 50:15 (NKJV), *Call upon Me in the day of trouble; I will deliver you, and you shall glorify Me.*

Psalm 84:11 (NASB), *For the LORD God is a sun and shield; The LORD gives grace and glory; No good thing does He withhold from those who walk uprightly.*

Isaiah 30:19b (NLT), *He will be gracious if you ask for help. He will surely respond to the sound of your cries.*

Jeremiah 33:3 (NASB), *Call to Me and I will answer you, and I will tell you great and mighty things, which you do not know.*

Matthew 18:19-20 (NASB), *Again I say to you, that if two of you agree on earth about anything that they may ask, it shall be done for them by My Father who is in heaven. For where two or three have gathered together in My name, there I am in their midst.*

Matthew 21:22 (AMP), *And whatever you ask for in prayer, having faith and [really] believing, you will receive.*

Luke 1:37 (AMP), *For with God nothing is ever impossible and no word from God shall be without power or impossible of fulfillment.*

Luke 11:13 (NASB), *If you then, being evil, know how to give good gifts to your children, how much more will your heavenly Father give the Holy Spirit to those who ask Him?*

John 14:13-14 (NLT), *You can ask for anything in my name, and I will do it, so that the Son can bring glory to the Father. Yes, ask me for anything in my name, and I will do it!*

John 15:7 (AMP), *If you live in Me [abide vitally united to Me] and My words remain in you and continue to live in your hearts, ask whatever you will, and it shall be done for you.*

John 16:24 (AMP), *Up to this time, you have not asked a [single] thing in My Name [as presenting all that I AM]; but now ask and keep on asking and you will receive, so that your joy (gladness, delight) may be full and complete.*

Hebrews 10:22-23 (NASB), *Let us draw near with a sincere heart in full assurance of faith, having our hearts sprinkled clean from an evil conscience and our bodies washed with pure water. Let us hold fast the confession of our hope without wavering, for He who promised is faithful.*

James 1:5-6 (NASB), *But if any of you lacks wisdom, let him ask of God, who gives to all generously and without reproach, and it will be given to him. But he must ask in faith without any doubting, for the one who doubts is like the surf of the sea, driven and tossed by the wind.*

James 5:16 (NLT), *Confess your sins to each other and pray for each other so that you may be healed. The earnest prayer of a righteous person has great power and produces wonderful results.*

I John 3:21-23 (NASB), *Beloved, if our heart does not condemn us, we have confidence before God; and whatever we ask we receive from Him, because we keep His commandments and do the things that are pleasing in His sight. This is His commandment, that we believe in the name of His Son Jesus Christ, and love one another, just as He commanded us.*

I John 5:14-15 (NASB), *This is the confidence which we have before Him, that, if we ask anything according to His will, He hears us. And if we know that He hears us in whatever we ask, we know that we have the requests which we have asked from Him.*

Words and Deeds

*W*hile the purpose of Moms in Prayer International is to pray, some groups choose to reach out to the school with written notes, goodies or gifts that we call Words and Deeds. Encouraging and supporting the school staff in this way is an optional activity of Moms in Prayer. Remember: We are not to evangelize by sending gifts or messages with Scripture, Christian slogans, etc. Words and Deeds should never be a burden to the group either financially or in time commitment, and the permission of the principal is required.

It is important for a group to be well established before the leader introduces Moms in Prayer to the principal. A personal visit is recommended. Here are some suggested points to cover:

- Acknowledge your appreciation of the principal's leadership and the tremendous responsibility that he/she has.

- Share your concern for the pressures that young people are facing today.

- Let the principal know that you belong to a group of moms called Moms in Prayer International who meet weekly to support the school through prayer.

- Indicate that your group of moms would like to bring treats at different times throughout the year to encourage and show appreciation to the faculty and staff.

If a principal declines your offer, thank him/her graciously, present a card with your name and phone number, and ask him/her to call you if there ever is a time when the staff might benefit from some encouragement.

Samples of encouragement and additional ideas are available in the *Leader's Guide & Personal Quiet Time.*

Statement of Faith

1. We believe the Bible to be inspired by the Holy Spirit, the only infallible, authoritative Word of God in all matters of faith and conduct.

   Deuteronomy 4:2; Psalm 19:7-9; Proverbs 30:5-6; I Corinthians 2:13; Galatians 1:8-9; II Timothy 3:15-17; II Peter 1:20-21; Revelation 22:18-19

2. We believe that there is one God, eternally existent in three persons: Father, Son and Holy Spirit.

   Genesis 1:1-3; Isaiah 44:6-8; Matthew 28:19-20; Mark 12:29; John 1:1-4; Acts 5:3-4; II Corinthians 13:14

3. We believe in God the Father, an infinite, personal spirit, perfect in holiness, wisdom, power and love. We believe that He concerns Himself mercifully in the affairs of each person, that He hears and answers prayer, and that He saves from sin and death all who come to Him through Jesus Christ.

   Genesis 21:33; Exodus 33:14; II Samuel 24:14; Isaiah 40:28; Jeremiah 31:3, 32:17; John 4:24; Romans 5:8, 11:33-34; Ephesians 1:19-20; I John 5:14-15; Revelation 4:8

4. We believe in God the Son, Jesus Christ the Savior, the only begotten Son of God, in His deity, in His virgin birth, in His sinless life, in His miracles, in His substitutionary and atoning death through His shed blood, in His bodily resurrection, in His ascension to the right hand of the Father, in His continuous intercession for His people, and in His personal return in power and in glory.

   Matthew 24:30; Mark 8:38; Luke 1:34-35, 24:27; John 1:1-2, 14, 18, 3:16; Romans 3:23-26, 8:34; I Corinthians 15:3-4; Hebrews 4:15

5. We believe in God the Holy Spirit, the Helper and Comforter, in His daily guidance and revelation of truth, in His conviction of sin, righteousness and judgment, and in His indwelling presence at the moment of salvation, enabling believers to live godly lives.

   John 3:5-8, 14:16-17, 16:13-14; Acts 1:8; I Corinthians 12:13; Ephesians 4:30-32, 5:18

6. We believe that everyone is born with a sinful nature, separated from God and in need of salvation. Regeneration by the Holy Spirit is absolutely essential for salvation through the repentance from sin and the acceptance of Jesus Christ as Lord and Savior.

   John 3:5-8, 5:24; Acts 2:21; Ephesians 1:6-7, 2:8-9; Titus 3:5; I Peter 1:23

7. We believe in the resurrection of both the saved and the lost; the saved unto the resurrection of eternal life and the lost unto the resurrection of eternal damnation.

   Luke 16:19-26; II Corinthians 5:8; Philippians 1:23; II Thessalonians 1:7-9; Revelation 20:11-15

8. We believe in the spiritual unity of believers in our Lord Jesus Christ.

   Acts 2:42-47; Romans 15:5-6; I Corinthians 12:12-13; Ephesians 4:3-6

Again I say to you, that if two of you agree on earth about anything that they may ask, it shall be done for them by My Father who is in heaven. For where two or three have gathered together in My name, there I am in their midst.

Matthew 18:19-20 (NASB)

Policies

*E*ach group is responsible to adhere to the policies of Moms in Prayer International. They are NOT optional.

1. Any individual or group not adhering to the Moms in Prayer International Statement of Faith or Policies shall not have the right to use the Moms in Prayer name or logo, nor represent the ministry in any manner.

2. Moms in Prayer International is not a lobbying group, regardless of how worthy the cause. Participation in outside political and social issues must be done solely on an individual basis. Under no circumstances should the Moms in Prayer name be used in conjunction with outside issues.

3. Confidentiality brings integrity to the ministry; therefore, all prayer requests must be held in strictest confidence.

4. Moms in Prayer groups are not to hold their meetings on public school campuses. We pray *for* the schools, not *in* the schools.

5. Moms in Prayer groups are not to solicit prayer requests nor place a prayer request box in any public school facility.

6. Moms in Prayer groups are not to use the public schools to solicit membership.

7. Unauthorized use of the Moms in Prayer name or logo is prohibited. It is the trademark of the Moms in Prayer International ministry, and its use requires the express, written permission of Moms in Prayer International.

8. Moms in Prayer rosters are for ministry use only. Under no circumstances are they to be used by, loaned to or shared with any other individual, organization, business or outside group.

9. No form of advertisement may be placed inside or on any Moms in Prayer International materials.

10. During group time, to allow for conversational, one accord prayer while following the Four Steps of Prayer, refrain from speaking in tongues out loud, praying the rosary or using contemplative prayer practices, which can include meditation that encourages the emptying of one's mind, prayer labyrinths, breath prayers (saying one word repetitively) and centering prayers (use of a mantra).

11. Moms in Prayer groups are not to engage in gossip or any conversation of a critical nature.

12. Moms in Prayer groups are specifically for women.

Don't worry about anything; instead, pray about everything. Tell God what you need, and thank him for all he has done.
Then you will experience God's peace, which exceeds anything we can understand. His peace will guard your hearts and minds as you live in Christ Jesus.

Philippians 4:6-7 (NLT)

Group Types

*M*oms in Prayer International offers a variety of group types. Please be sure to register your group, designating the specific type of group, and list ALL the schools being prayed for on a regular basis during the School Concerns intercession time. For more information about which schools to register, please see the online page Praying for More Than One School under Leader's Corner at www.MomsInPrayer.org.

In keeping with the mission of Moms in Prayer International, groups which pray for children who are not students will choose a school to pray for, possibly a child's future or previous school, or another school in the area which does not have its own Moms in Prayer group. Then, during the school intercession time, the group will pray for the teachers, administrators, support staff and students at the chosen school(s).

To register your group, please fill out the form at the back of this *Moms in Prayer Booklet* or visit www.MomsInPrayer.org/Register.

Traditional: The traditional Moms in Prayer group prays for a specific school. If praying for more than one school, please register all the schools being prayed for on a regular basis during the School Concerns time.

College/University: Mothers of college students find prayer is a special way to connect with a college student, whether living away or remaining at home.

Career: Mothers of adult children who are no longer in school can still be praying for this important season in their child's life.

Grandmothers: Grandmothers can pray with a group for the school their grandchildren attend or they can form a Grandmothers Group. Several schools and all ages of children may be represented.

Church-based: Women in a local community may choose to meet together in an area church to pray for their children and the schools they attend. Several schools and all ages of children may be represented.

Children with Special Needs: Mothers who have children with special needs often pray in Traditional or Church-based Groups. However, for moms who wish to pray specifically with those who understand the uniqueness of raising a child with special needs, they can form a Children with Special Needs Group. When registering online, please choose the group type "Special Needs."

Homeschool: Homeschool moms are in a unique position to pray for themselves as both teacher and mom.

Language-based: Moms who come together based on a language other than English, such as Spanish, Korean or Chinese, can register as a Language-based Group.

Military: Mothers with sons or daughters in the military may choose to pray with a Career Group or form their own Military Group.

Preschool: A Preschool Group can be a group praying for children who attend preschool, or it can be a group praying for children not yet attending school.

Prison/Jail: Some Moms in Prayer leaders minister to moms in prison or jail by facilitating an hour of prayer for the children these moms so desperately miss.

Prodigal: Mothers of wayward children can feel isolated and distraught. Meeting to pray with other moms can bring hope as together the children are lifted to the Lord. Moms of children not walking with the Lord can form a Prodigal Group or can pray with any relevant group type.

Working Moms: Moms who work outside the home can pray together before work, at lunch, after work or on the weekend.

Frequently Asked Questions

1. **How do I find another mom to pray with?**

   First, make sure your group is registered so other moms can find you on the Moms in Prayer Group Locator.

   Most people join a group because they were invited by a friend. For this reason, a variety of flyers are available online under www.MomsInPrayer.org/LeadersCorner. These can be personalized and printed to share with other women at church, in your neighborhood or elsewhere. (Please remember not to publicize your group on a public school campus.)

   A Get the Word Out section is also available online under Leaders Corner with banners, videos, press releases and more!

2. **How do I ensure that my group continues after I leave?**

   We pray that every group will continue until Jesus returns. Please be intentional about training a co-leader or co-leaders who can fill in for you when you or your child are sick or out of town, and who might be willing to pick up the baton of leadership from you if God calls you to another school/group. If you lead a traditional group that prays for one school, be praying for your group's next leader and give the women with younger children an opportunity to lead the group occasionally, so they will be comfortable doing so when your child(ren) changes schools.

3. **How can I have the most effective prayer time?**

   Pray throughout the week for your group. During the Moms in Prayer hour, use the Four Steps format, praying in one accord, agreement prayer.

   A Moms in Prayer group prays for their children and concerns that pertain to their school. Topics other than these must be prayed about before or after the prayer hour.

   Moms with more than one child at the same school are encouraged to focus on one child each week. This allows for more concentrated and specific prayer for that child during the given time for intercession. Moms may alternate children weekly or focus on one child for several weeks or months.

If a mom has a specific prayer request for the school, she is to give it to the leader before the meeting. This will avoid unnecessary discussion during prayer time as well as give the leader an opportunity to consider if it is appropriate for sharing with the group for prayer.

A mom who knows a teacher personally and is confident that the teacher is a Christian may ask for prayer requests privately. To protect the student's privacy, the teacher should never give the student's name when sharing a personal prayer request.

4. **As a Moms in Prayer mom, how do I handle personal school-related issues?**

   The Moms in Prayer ministry must not be used in addressing any personal issues when dealing with the school. Should a Moms in Prayer mom find it necessary to go to a teacher or principal concerning a child or a school-related matter, she is to go with a gracious spirit as a concerned parent without identifying herself as being part of Moms in Prayer.

5. **What does it mean to be a part of Moms in Prayer International?**

   Moms in Prayer International is a worldwide prayer movement. God is calling moms from Norway to New Zealand, from El Salvador to Ethiopia, to gather in united prayer for their children and schools. The hearts of moms beat the same all over the world.

   For more information about what God is doing in this international ministry, visit www.MomsinPrayer.org/AroundTheWorld.

6. **How can my group support the worldwide ministry of Moms in Prayer International?**

   You can support Moms in Prayer through your prayers. Prayer requests are available at www.MomsInPrayer.org/MinistryRequests and /AroundTheWorld.

   You can also support Moms in Prayer International through your financial gifts. Many groups donate to the ministry in order to mobilize the women of the world to come together and pray, so they, too, can experience the peace and hope that comes with corporate prayer. For more information, please visit www.MomsInPrayer.org/Donate.

*May he grant your heart's desires
and make all your plans succeed.
May we shout for joy when we hear of your victory
and raise a victory banner in the name of our God.
May the LORD answer all your prayers.*

Psalm 20:4-5 (NLT)

Registration Form

(Please print legibly.)

Name _____

Address _____

City _____

State/Province/Zip _____

Country _____

E-mail _____

Home Phone _____

Cell Phone _____

I am a: ☐ Group Leader   ☐ Potential Leader

☐ Group Member   ☐ Not in a group

☐ Other _____

If you are a group leader or potential leader, please fill out the following information:

School(s) being prayed for _____

_____

School District(s) _____

School County _____

Type of Group (See page 26.) _____

Mail completed Registration Form to:

Moms in Prayer International
P.O. Box 1120, Poway, CA 92074-1120

You may also register at www.MomsInPrayer.org.